Living
IN THE WAIT

HOW TO USE THE DELAYS
IN LIFE DIFFERENTLY

Melissa Vande Kieft

Cover Design: Story Seven and UpFrame Creative
Lead Writer: Melissa Vande Kieft
Editor: Marguerite Bonnett and Angela Tewalt
Proofing Editor & Publishing Manager: Renee Rebnord and Carrie Kuhl

Throne Publishing Group
1601 East 69th St N Suite 306
Sioux Falls, SD 57108

PRAISE FOR
Living in the Wait

"*Living in the Wait* is not a fluffy how-to guide filled with stories on how waiting makes you stronger. Instead, this is a book that shares Melissa's real-life experience and heartache — pointing us back to Jesus at every turn. Waiting can be so hard, but Melissa teaches us how to wait well, because she's been there."

—**ADAM WEBER,** lead pastor of Embrace Church and author of *Love Has a Name*

"Learning how to live during seasons of waiting can be one of the hardest things we do in life. We're left questioning and wondering so much about ourselves, our purpose, and God, leaving us unsure what to do next. Melissa has written a heartfelt and practical guide for us to follow during these in-between times. She has walked this hard road herself, and what God has done in and through her is a testimony for us all!"

— **JENNIFER DUKES LEE,** author of *Growing Slow*, speaker, and writer for Dayspring's (in)courage

"As someone who's navigated many seasons of waiting, I found the words on each page so healing. Reading this book, I felt like I was having a conversation with a trusted friend. One who lovingly understood and made me feel safe during what's typically an uncertain and vulnerable time. Melissa is special, and you'll be so much better for getting to know her through her words. I know I am."

— **HOLLY CHRISTINE HAYES,** founder + CEO of Sanctuary Project and author of *From Basement to Sanctuary*

"With a culture that does all it can to instantly get what it wants, Melissa kindly and graciously guides her readers to find the blessings in disguise that can be uncovered during our seasons of waiting. It's a must-read for anyone who finds themselves wondering what good can come from the delays in life."

— **BRITTNEY MOSES,** mental health & wellness advocate and host of The Faith & Mental Wellness Podcast

"This book is a practical, inspiring, tender companion for anyone who finds themselves in a period of waiting without knowing. Melissa so beautifully illustrates how all of the messiness of waiting — the pain, hope, heartache, grief, faith, and fear — can be transformed from a devastating cacophony into an exquisite symphony that elevates not only she who waits, but all those who are ultimately inspired by what God is able to bring forth when we choose to live in the wait."

— **ANNA SAUCIER,** business + life coach and founder of Cycle Power Summit & Unexplained Infertility Summit

"Walking through a season of waiting requires a community. Surrounding ourselves with others who can share hope, a way through, and a reminder of the breakthrough on the other side. I'm so grateful to Melissa for coming alongside us all to do exactly that."

—**ANNIE MOSS,** founder of The Vintage Sparrow, speaker, and author

"Waiting isn't for sissies, and it will either make you or break you if you let it. But, as Melissa shares in her practical and vulnerable new book, when you put the control in God's hands, He will lead you through every time. She tells it like it is in her no-holds-barred narrative, giving wise counsel for others who are grappling with any type of waiting."

— **KATE BATTISTELLI,** author of *The God Dare*, speaker, mentor, and co-host of The Mom to Mom Podcast

"Having someone to support, encourage, and guide you during difficult seasons of life is essential. Melissa knows firsthand what it's like to live life with unmet desires and most importantly, knows how to help you live life to the fullest during them because of who God is."

—**DR. CHERYL BONES,** DC, IFMCP, founder of Prairie Roots Chiropractic & Functional Medicine and The Wellness Collective

"On each page, Melissa's authentic faith, humor and vulnerability will challenge and encourage your heart. Thank you, Melissa, for taking us by the hand and showing us how to live in the wait."

—**NICOLE CLARK**, founder of Twelve 12 Ministries and Called and Encouraged

"Sitting on the front row, I watched a giant come against all the ways Melissa knew how to function and threatened to take her out. It was a messy battle, but the giant came out on the short end of the fight! I am learning a lot about God's timing — how he comforts, refines, and develops us "In the Wait" — watching Melissa transform through this journey. I am excited that she is sharing the hard-earned wisdom she has won with the world and pray God speaks light into your darkness through this book!"

— **BRUCE JOHNSON,** Pastor and Fellowship of Christian Athletes character coach

"Melissa talks to you in such a way that you believe what she's writing is about you, because it is. She cares about each and every person she connects with. Not only is Melissa a really genuine person, she has this gentle, authentic way of reaching into the shadowy parts of your soul that are hurt and angry, and she helps you to pull them out and heal them."

—**EMILY POGUE,** writer, editor, and epic storyteller

To my guy, Ry

I know this story is one we never wanted to write, but I'm beyond grateful it was you beside me the entire time.

We did this together.

To my daughter, Crosbee

You, the very being and intricacies that God molded together to create you, are the most beautiful design I've ever seen.

All that you are, is exactly who you're supposed to be.

The depths of love I have for you are immeasurable.

I'm so grateful I get to know you.

The Wait List

The following have been submitted by people from all over the world. They bravely shared what they're waiting for in hopes that you, the reader, would take a moment to lift them and their request up in prayer. Praying for other people is about community, and as someone who's picked up this book, you're now part of the family. In Habakkuk 2:2, Jesus shares the importance of writing down our dreams. These requests are listed so we can witness God's faithfulness unfold. Imagine one day opening up this book, years later after your season of waiting has passed, now standing in the newness God has provided.

Thank you for taking the time to open your heart and say a prayer for those on The Wait List.

My season of singleness has been something I have struggled with the past few years as relationships form and marriages take place around me. I long for that time in my story. — *Aryca L.*

We are praying to conceive baby No. 2. — *Natalie B.*

A miracle from God. God to place his healing hands on my husband who was diagnosed with a grade 4 brain tumor (GMB). For my girls to have their daddy as they grow up. — *Katie B.*

100+ acres of wide-open land on which to raise my sons. — *Jeremy B.*

Maybe I'll get pregnant again, but even if I don't, God is still good. I'll continue waiting to meet my baby in heaven. — *Ashley C.*

My wait is my weight. My desire is to feel lighter, healthier, and more energetic. And to stop feeling like no matter what I do, it never works. I want my body to be a testament to God's grace and glory. — *Marguerite B.*

Still waiting for the Man He has for me! Not because I need a man, but because I want to share my life with the Man God designed for me! — *Charia A.*

Another baby. We currently have a 4-year-old daughter who wants nothing more than to be a big sister, and we want another child to love. — *Amanda K.*

An old house with amazing woodwork and a front porch to enjoy God's amazing sunrises. Then fix the old barn to become my "she shed". — *Stuart K*

I am praying for a happy healthy marriage and to adopt a child. —*Jamie T.*

A cure to metastatic breast cancer. I have been very lucky to have treatments that are keeping it at bay but no cure. — *Cheryl P.*

Waiting to start our family. Waiting to stop waiting. — *Stephanie B.*

Ability to understand and balance being a supportive and empathetic wife to someone with chronic pain, a mother and haven to a special needs child, and self-care. —*Jonalee D.*

Freedom from severe allergies. — *Chris T.*

For over 2 years, I thought I was waiting to get pregnant and become a mom, but now I realize I am waiting for an answer about God's plan for our family. — *Ana M.*

I am waiting for my life partner to manifest as I have a deep desire to start a family and have children. — *Nora D.*

We pray for protection, complete healing, full recovery, and happiness for Rosie and her family. These 2 marathons haven't been easy for Rosie and her family. — *Cassandra K.*

Having babies. — *Silvia E.*

For our dream home that will provide a safe place to make memories and build relationships. — *Missy K.*

As a mom and spouse of a Type 1 Diabetic, I have been on The Wait List for a cure for many, many years. I pray for patience as I wait and a cure to be found very soon! — *Sara W.*

We are waiting for the Lord to fulfill this deep desire to grow our family. — *Rebekah M.*

My season of singleness to be over. My strong desire to experience life with someone & start a family feels so distant. — *Samantha M.*

We are currently waiting for the beginning of our family on earth. Our angel baby Ezra Joseph has helped make it possible to be on this journey with our rainbow baby. — *Shelby S.*

I'm waiting for the godly husband God is preparing for me. At 34 years old, I'm concerned marriage, even parenthood, may not happen for me. — *Kari H.*

Contents

Introduction

Have you ever been traveling along the road of life – smooth and carefree – certain of where you're going and what to expect?

With the warm wind blowing through your hair and dance music pumping through the speakers, you're full of excitement and possibility for all that lies ahead. The straight and flat highway stretches beneath you, making the trip easy to navigate. Being the only car cruising this direction, there's no cause for concern. Even better, there's no road construction to slow you down or send you on a detour.

Your confidence grows with each passing mile, as the anticipation of what's to come gets closer and closer. What you long for, your final destination, is something you can see clearly in your mind and feel strongly in your heart.

Unexpectedly, the scenery begins to darken, and a chilly wind begins to blow. The highway starts to narrow, becoming increasingly hilly and curvy. Up ahead, you see something on the paved road. At first, it appears small, manageable to bypass, but as you get closer, the situation comes into full view. A massive tree blocks the entire road making it impossible to keep going. Just your luck, you're the first person at the scene.

As you process the situation, the plans you put in place start to dissipate when you realize where you want to go might not be an option anymore. Disappointment and fear begin to settle in. This delay has interrupted your schedule, and you're scrambling to figure out what's next.

You know your final destination and what it looks like, but how to get there has drastically changed. The journey has taken a turn for the worse, or so you believe, and you're not sure if you'll ever get there.

This is *not* how you imagined your road trip would be like.

"What do I do now?" you cry out.

This is a mile marker moment.

You know, the ones that leave a thick, black mark on our timeline of life. They often are seen as either "good" or "bad". Either way, they're defining and move us in different directions, whether we want them to or not.

My mile marker moment happened in October, and while I don't remember the exact date, the scene and message became one of those moments for me.

A major roadblock had appeared in my life and sidetracked my plans, taking me on a long and winding detour. The whole idea of waiting, its purpose, and how to live in it, kept coming to the surface. This transition time had captivated my heart, and I wanted to dig deeper.

You see, at that point, I'd been living in a state of limbo for many years. This in-between time is something we all experience, and yet, we don't get to choose the things in life we wait for nor how long our seasons of waiting will last. We all have unmet desires, places where we feel God has not listened, answered, or given us what we want.

I didn't know it at the time, but Jesus was pruning me in my wait. He was cutting down the dead and overgrown branches on my heart and mind that were holding me back and limiting my potential. It was a necessary ritual for greater growth and a more fruitful life. [1] Oddly enough, it was those dead sticks that brought me new life.

Through that process, He revealed seven truths that kept me grounded during my season of waiting, even to this day.

W.orship
A.cceptance
I.nvestigate
T.rust
I.ntentional
N.ew
G.enerosity

Putting these principles into practice is our prep plan for Living in the Wait and helps set the stage for experiencing and seeing God's faithfulness firsthand.

They will help you rewrite the narrative, the story you're telling yourself, and ultimately what you're living and believing.

At their core, all of these provide some level of healing, coping, and hope. They're not instant but the formation of a new habit, which requires continual and consistent practice for results and change to happen. These strategies pivot your perspective on your situation, which creates the freedom and desire to live in the wait.

Applying these truths won't suddenly move the tree from your road and set you off on your way. Instead, they teach you how to plant the seeds during any season of waiting, making way for growth and your ability to bear fruit. Allow these revelations to help your roots grow deep to keep you firmly planted in Jesus as you navigate the in-between.

Waiting is not a one-size-fits-all type of thing. What these truths look like in your own life may vary, and that's okay. Maybe a few resonate with you and the rest you throw out or adapt. The most important thing is that you now feel you have some sort of direction and control during this time.

Use these truths to live in your wait and use delays in life differently.

I invite you to join me at The Truth Tree.

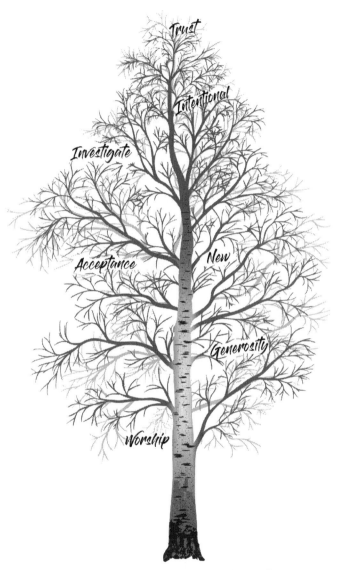

"I am the vine, you are the branches."
John 15:5

Section 1
WEARY AND WORN

"Our willingness to wait, reveals the value we place
on the object we're waiting for."

— *C.S. Lewis*—

— CHAPTER ONE —

Beg, Buy, or Bypass

WE ALL EXPERIENCE IT

The truth is, we all wait. I didn't write those rules, and just because we may not like them, doesn't make them any less true.

It's something we all experience, and yet, we don't get to choose the things in life we wait for nor how long our seasons of waiting will last.

Many times, this situation isn't immediately resolved, and we grow impatient. We become frustrated and do everything we can to get the outcome we want. We start to question ourselves and doubt our identity, value, and worth.

The longing grows greater and deeper, and we're left wondering, "How do I continue living while waiting for my heart's desire?"

For many of you, this place might sound all too familiar. It's a place you can clearly visualize because you're currently walking that path. Friend, I'm a witness to your pain.

I walked a very similar road. One I so desperately wanted to get off. To travel as fast as I could through it, so it would just be over. No meandering or getting lost on the trail for this girl. Straight

Waiting, "is when you have left the tried and true, but have not yet been able to replace it with anything else. It is when you are between your old comfort zone and any possible new answer. If you are not trained in how to hold anxiety, how to live with ambiguity, how to entrust and wait, you will run...anything to flee this terrible cloud of unknowing."

—Richard Rohr

and to the point, please. The middle, the in-between, and the not yet was no place for me.

These seasons are often referred to as "hell in the hallway." Yup, that about sums it up for me and how I feel about the ones I've endured. I've had my fill and am so over it. And yet, as I write this, I know in the depths of my soul, I will have countless more.

There are no words to truly express the depths of heartache, disappointment, and loss you may be feeling relative to the current situation you're experiencing. None of the words I share aim to fix or take that away. That's a job above my pay grade, reserved for the one and only Jesus.

At first glance, waiting would appear to be a passive activity. One where you, well, wait. Visions of people aimlessly looking around, nervously tapping their feet, wandering eyes, or mindless scrolling on phones.

- A waste of time
- Pointless

- An interruption
- Annoying
- An inconvenience

Because of that, waiting is often seen as having no value. We all know time is our greatest asset, so why would we want to spend it on the intermission?

You know what is the opposite of waiting? Instantaneous. We live in a world that is built on and prides itself on doing everything it can to avoid being put on hold. Think about it, we have Instagram, Instapots, express lanes, fast food, and rush orders.

We do everything we can to beg, bypass, or buy our way out of waiting.

Let's be real, we typically don't pencil waiting into our schedules.

And I get it.

Waiting is uncomfortable.

It's full of unknowns and uncertainty, and many of those are grounded in fear.

Sounds like just the place I want to hang out for days, months, even years, right?! Reminds me of Moses and the Israelites

Regardless of what you're waiting for, it matters.

wandering in the desert for forty years. [2] I wonder what Moses was thinking during that time.

The unknowns surrounding waiting can cause us fear because it reminds us that we aren't in control.

And that, my friends, is the heart of why waiting is so difficult.

Waiting is a loss of control.

And we don't like that. If we could control what was happening, we would eliminate the middle.

But the truth is, we need down time in our lives.

These seasons of waiting often happen when we don't want them, or they last longer than we prefer. Let's face it, periods of pause are not a glamorous topic to talk about, so the benefits are often dismissed.

Nonetheless, there are advantages to being still. Slowing down gives us time to rest, reflect, and most importantly, quiet all the noise so we can hear from God. These interim periods give us time to process what we're experiencing, which, I dare say, is exactly why we prefer to avoid them.

Hurrying from one thing to the next often leads to a state of busyness that blocks our ability to receive encouragement, hope, peace, and direction. All things people on The Wait List are searching for. [3]

Waiting is a loss of control.

It's important to mention, there will be times you'll feel a loss or void as you wait. And other times, you'll feel gratefulness and abundance. To me, that's an indicator of the type of season you're in.

Either way, you're waiting.

And regardless of what you're waiting for, it matters.

Because that desire you have in your heart was put there by God.

We're human and often compare ourselves to others thinking our request is insignificant or not as bad as what someone else is going through. This shuts down our ability to be open to what God can do in and through our lives. But know this, God doesn't compare what you're experiencing to someone else. He doesn't use the same measuring stick we use to decide if He should give your request attention.

There is no hierarchy in waiting, it's universal.

And regardless of the breakthrough you're hoping for, we can have the confidence to come to God with all our requests.

This might not be what you expected to hear, but seeing both sides of the coin is a valuable lesson in waiting.

"You will find that the long wait has done you some kind of good
which you would not have had otherwise."

— *C.S. Lewis*—

— CHAPTER TWO —

Sticks, Sticks, and Sticks

I PACKED THE WRONG CLOTHES

If you've ever walked up a hill, you know they typically have a more gradual ascent. Hills aren't too high nor too steep, and you can usually see the end. Sure, they can be difficult and require effort, but most of the time you can make it to the top.

The mile marker moment I'm about to share with you was my first mountain. Whether you've actually climbed a mountain or not, you're probably aware they're not the same as a hill. Mountains are steep and have a sharp incline. The trip to the top takes much more time. It requires an entirely different set of circumstances for which to prepare and plan. You wear certain clothes, and your packing list is much longer. The journey requires more effort, and oftentimes, the end is hidden from plain sight.

This was a mountain I was not yet prepared to climb.

POSTPONED PLANS

I've never been a fan of making decisions. My aversion to them is mainly because I never want to make the wrong choice. Growing up, my mom's response whenever I asked for her input about a decision I had to make was, "Listen to your heart." My quick reply was always, "I can't hear my heart!"

While this has felt true most of my life, one fall day something happened. The yard around the home my husband, Ry, and I live in has a lot of trees, and subsequently, we have a lot of fallen sticks and broken branches to pick up. One random October day, I was doing just that. Winter was just around the corner, the wind blowing, and leaves falling all around me. The weather was an accurate indicator of the swirling emotions I felt inside.

Stick after stick after stick, I picked them up and threw them in a pile. Each twig seemed to represent another thought or feeling I'd had since I was pushed into this season of waiting. While I was throwing the sticks at the ground, I might as well have been hurling them at God. Using them as a barrier to build a wall to protect myself from this nightmare that I blamed Him for putting me in. It was a way to shield myself from the pain this unmet desire was causing in my life.

Control has a not-so-funny way of creating a false sense of safety.

Ry and I were coming to a point in our lives where we needed to make a big decision – continue on our current path or forge a new one. We were two-and-a-half years into our infertility journey. Roughly 1,000 straight days of doing everything right, only to get nothing. We had no affirmation to point us in the direction that what we were doing had a glimmer or chance of giving us our desired outcome.

We were faced with something that appeared easy to control, and yet, staring back at us was a reality that seemed to mock our futile attempts of having any control. A friend of mine said it best, "I had never been presented with a situation that I couldn't find an answer to."

To say I felt angry, exhausted, and extremely hopeless would be an understatement. There are no words to truly convey the depths of despair I was feeling at that point.

The disappointment was a reality I could never escape, and yard work was yet another example of a simple task I couldn't do without the weight of what we were walking through invading my entire being. I felt trapped by the longing and ache that seemed to grow deeper and stronger each day we had to wait, infuriated by the feeling that God wasn't listening or willing to give us what we wanted.

The entire time I was doing this mundane chore, I was wrestling and talking with God. Pleading and begging Him to help me understand why I was living a life that wasn't going according to my plan. Why He was withholding my desires from me. Over and over and over, I cried out to Him. A continuous pattern, just like the repetition my body was experiencing with each branch I picked up.

The sticks were beginning to pile up by now. The weather was unchanging, the consistent ebb and flow of the wind, crashing into my body. But without warning, I felt a change. I was still performing this dull task, but something began to shift internally. It happened very subtly, but my questions to God unexpectedly morphed into: "How do I continue living while waiting for my heart's desire? How do I live in the wait?"

This new set of questions was on repeat in my heart, when suddenly, I heard it. It was so faint I had to stop to reflect on what had just whispered through my body.

I had no idea that what I had just experienced, this stick moment, would lead to my biggest breakthrough, in more ways than one.

To truly understand how I got to that moment, I need to take you back. Back to the day I lost all control and began my more than three-year season of waiting.

———————————

If you had been a fly on the wall that September day, you would've seen what it looks like to have someone's hopes and dreams instantly disappear. It was Ry's and my first appointment with a Reproductive Endocrinologist, roughly one year and three months after we started "trying" to have a family. Not that I was counting or anything.

The multiple hours-long appointment was a montage of countless tests, and after all the poking and prodding, we were

"How do I continue living while waiting for my heart's desire? How do I live in the wait?"

finally given the diagnosis of unexplained infertility. Despite this verdict, my gut told me, and would continue to tell me months and years later, something else was going on; there's more to the story. While that first appointment was information overload, for me, it was more than that. It was identity overload.

I remember looking out the window, sobbing as we drove home, our car speeding along the interstate. The plans I had for my life, literally flew out the window, disappearing into the rearview mirror with each passing mile. The picture I had imagined for my life had become so unclear. My expectation of that journey no longer matched my reality.

Control has a not-so-funny way of creating a false sense of safety and I found myself no longer feeling safe in my own story. The control I thought I had over this outcome in my life, no longer existed. It was such a helpless and hopeless feeling to a level I had never experienced before. That appointment was the beginning of a loss that God would work to turn into a gain over the next couple of years.

A Myers-Briggs test the Spring of my sophomore year at Morningside College set me up on a career path as an Event Planner. I knew instantly from the description this was exactly who I was supposed to be. Little did I know at the ripe old age of 20 that this career choice would establish a need, desire, and identity rooted in control.

Because we're friends, and friends tell each other the truth, I have to share that I'm a total Type A person. And being an event planner compounded things. It's a fun gig, but with that comes a lot of responsibility. The main one is to keep everything under control and plan for the unexpected. To foresee what others can't and avoid unplanned situations as much as possible. I've been planning events for over 15 years and with that comes the false perception of being really good at controlling things.

Note: That did not always lend itself well to my personal life.

I would later learn the reason this season was so difficult. The heart of who I was when we began trying to expand our family was a planner. I control what seemingly can't be controlled.

I had tied my identity to being in control, and this situation was flirting with my biggest fear: feeling out of control. It wasn't a formal ceremony, with an exchange of vows or rings, but that fear and I were definitely united in a not so holy matrimony.

Maybe you can relate. You've created this picture in your heart and mind of what your life might look like. But right now, that expectation doesn't match your reality.

The image you envisioned is something you feel to the core of who you are and represents more than what meets the eye. The sum of all the parts of this portrait embodies the experiences, memories, fulfillment, and opportunities you wish to have. This picture represents the ability to bring said desires into your life and what those experiences can provide, bring, or give. It's about so much more than just the thing you're waiting for.

In this place, we catch ourselves repeatedly saying, "This isn't how it's supposed to be. Change it God, change it."

Section 2

HOPE AND HEALING

"The Lord is not slow to fulfill his promise as some count slowness, but is patient toward you."

— *2 Peter 3:9 ESV*—

— CHAPTER THREE —

Our Example of Waiting

JESUS WAITED

If waiting is something we all experience, does that mean Jesus experienced it too?

Jesus was sent to earth to die on the cross and through His death and resurrection, we can have eternal life. He knew what His purpose was, but until that was fulfilled, He was on earth, waiting.

He shared the Gospel, performed miracles, brought healing, and gave people life! The list of all the ways He actively lived life to the fullest during his 30 plus years goes on and on.

Jesus is our ultimate example of Living in the Wait!

Ultimately, He used that time to teach us how to be more like Christ. This is exactly what these transitional times can do in our own lives.

He also showed us that these seasons of waiting might not be all sunshine and rainbows. While He was here, Jesus was persecuted, mocked, ridiculed, questioned, and doubted.

While it may be painful to know He experienced this and so will we, this is also great news for us on The Wait List. Jesus experienced waiting firsthand, so He totally understands what we're going through. This means we can boldly go to Him with all our fears, disappointments, and heartaches. All of it! And, while our wait may be different than His, He reassures us, through His own experience, we're not alone. It doesn't eliminate what you're experiencing or instantly bring you your breakthrough, but it can provide hope, healing, and peace.

When I learned this, waiting was no longer this unfair, punishing part of life. The best way I can describe it is that it became normal in a way. Because Jesus waited, it makes sense that we will too. I mention Jesus' waiting not to compare ourselves to Him, but to relate to Him. He completely and wholeheartedly understands waiting.

PROTECTION IN THE WAIT

I've often wondered about this idea of living life while knowing our fate like Jesus did.

If I would've known at the very beginning of our marriage that we were going to experience this type of wait, I would have done things differently. But I think not knowing all the ins and outs of our lives is Jesus' way of protecting us.

If Jesus waited, it makes sense that we will too.

I can remember saying to God, "If you could just tell me the outcome, regardless of how long, I would be willing to wait. I'll wait as long as you want, just as long as I know I will get there." Who am I kidding, y'all? I was bargaining with God to reveal my future to me. Knowing what we may or may not face, or the outcome of those situations, doesn't make them any easier to live through.

I think of Jesus from that perspective. I wonder what He thought, waking up day after day, knowing He was one day closer to His horrible death on the cross. Can you imagine going through life knowing and waiting for your timer to go off? I speak for myself when I say I'm not sure I would've been able to get up day after day and generously pour into others like He did.

Thank you, Jesus, for sparing us from knowing what's ahead. You protect us from the unplanned things that life brings so we can focus on living life to the fullest and be used by you.

What I do gather from His life and death is that if He can do what He did during His lifetime of waiting, we can, too. We have the same power inside us, but I think it's often easier to not use it.[4] Instead, we tend to rely on the world and what it has to offer regarding our circumstances.

I don't share this to make light of any situation in your life. While the theme of our wait might not be the same, we're human and heartache is universal. The reason I share this is to bring you hope. To show you an example to follow that can provide a way through the wait. How He's going to do it, only God knows. So, I encourage you to go to Him and ask how you're supposed to live in the wait. He'll answer you, just like He did me.

NOT ON BREAK

When our dreams are delayed for months, years, and decades, it's easy to lose faith and hope. It's like, God, are you even listening to me? Hello, anybody home?

Remember this, God is not on break in your wait.

He's actually quite the opposite. He's very active, which is why He encourages us to do the same.

It's important for us to know and understand this, because it's a reflection in our own lives. If we can grasp these concepts and allow them to slowly take root in our lives, our outlook can't help but be changed.

I love details, which works out great being an event planner. For each event I coordinate, I create a document I call my "Play by Play" that lists every aspect about the event. I imagine God sitting in Heaven graciously holding each of our personal play by play documents. Just like I plan and coordinate the details of an event to make it successful, God wants to do the same in your life, because He loves and cares for you beyond measure. Creating, orchestrating, designing, and implementing details are God's specialty. [5] He wants to be involved in every part of our lives, no matter how big or small. He cares about them all.

Knowing God is in the details can bring comfort and reassurance during our transition times. Do I know what He's working on or doing? Not always, but I don't have to. He does, and I trust Him to work it out. I've seen Him do that in multiple areas of my life before and know He'll do it again. This doesn't mean it'll fit my

Remember this, God is not on break in your wait.

timeline or expectations, though. There's a proper time for His plans to unfold and only God knows when. [6]

Whatever season of waiting you're in, He cares. There might be many moving parts, which take longer to coordinate, but He's meticulously working, planning, and organizing every detail so when it arrives in your life, it's exactly as it should be. He loves you, and you can trust Him with the desires of your heart. How do I know this? He's the one who gave them to you in the first place.

A LIFETIME OF WAITING

The whole reason Jesus came to earth was for you and me. By dying on the cross, He took on the sin of the world so we could live life to the fullest.

And yet, He's still waiting:

- To heal our hearts
- To trust Him
- To have a personal relationship with Him
- To be obedient to His plans

He experiences the pain of waiting when His children refuse a relationship with Him, deny who He is, and have hardened their hearts to Him.

Why is this important to know?

Our eternal life depends on it.

Until each and every person confesses their sins and accepts Jesus as their Savior, He will continue to wait for us. He loves us so much that He's willing to wait years, decades, sometimes entire lifetimes for His children to come to Him. There will come a time when the world ends, and Jesus won't be waiting anymore. Please, don't wait until it's too late.

It's much easier to blame Jesus for making us wait, instead of going to Him. We're upset with Him because our plans and expectations are not happening according to our timeline. I get it. I've lived with that anger. But you guys, Jesus wants nothing more than for us to go to Him during our times of uncertainty to transform our hearts and show us how we can live in the wait.

The fact that Jesus is still waiting (present tense) means He gets it. He understands all the thoughts, feelings, and conflicting emotions that revolve around waiting. He knows what it feels like to have your heart physically broken Every. Single. Day. He has those same feelings when it comes to us accepting or rejecting Him as our Savior.

Jesus is waiting for you today. Please, don't make Him wait any longer. [7]

Jesus wants nothing more than for us to go to Him during our times of uncertainty to transform our hearts and show us how we can live in the wait.

"We must be willing to let go of the life we've planned, so as to have the life that is waiting for us."

—*Joseph Campbell*—

— CHAPTER FOUR —

Rewriting the Narrative

FLIPPING THE COIN

We often think there is nothing we can do during our wait, but the truth is, there *is* something we can do.

What if these delays in life are our invitation to use that time differently? To flip the coin and rewrite the narrative we've been told these holding patterns represent in our lives. Not necessarily changing them from bad to good, but more from:

- Pointless to preparation
- Worthless to valuable
- Stagnant to growth
- Wasting time to transformation
- Hopeless to hopeful

Please know, nothing I share here is to diminish, dismiss, or belittle what you're experiencing. It. Is. Hard. I'm here to validate your pain and loss. I wholeheartedly understand and know with every fiber of my being how dark of a place you're in and how awful it feels. I see you.

But I'm your friend, and that means sometimes we all need a little help flipping the coin to see what's on the other side.

Think of a penny. When life seems like it's been put on hold, it's so easy to stare endlessly at one side of that coin. Wishing, hoping, and wanting it to look differently. You can scrub, paint, and scratch all you want, but Honest Abe will still be looking back at you.

Flipping the coin doesn't remove what's on the other side. It's still there, but now you have a different perspective. Not just yours, but Jesus'. Until you deliberately turn that coin over, you don't know what's on the other side.

When your desires are deferred, it's so easy to only see one side of the story — yours. But know this, God views it differently. Allow Him to change the way you see your wait and yourself because friend, His view provides life, freedom, and hope.

To be vulnerable with you, I understand the idea of flipping that coin can sound exhausting. It feels like starting over and taking every ounce of energy you have to flip it. And I agree with you. So instead of shouldering that on your own, let's ask someone to help.

Allow Him to change the way you see your wait and yourself because friend, His view provides life, freedom, and hope.

THE FRENCH BRAID

My aunt is a retired hairstylist and has given me almost every haircut I've ever had, except for that one time I was a hair model and they dyed my hair orange. [8] When I was little and we would get together with her, I'd always ask her to French braid my hair. I thought it was the coolest thing. She taught me well, as I can now braid my own hair.

The French braid technique starts with three strands of hair at the top of your head. As you braid, you continually pick up and grab additional pieces of hair, crisscrossing and intertwining strand after strand, until there's none left to grab.

When we go about our seasons of waiting without Jesus, you might start with three strands consisting of disappointment, heartache, and frustration. As you continue, you might pick up anger, loneliness, and hopelessness. This intertwining of emotions can continue for months, even years. While you still get the end product of a braid, the journey is a depletion of energy, leaving you unable to enjoy what was just created.

By inviting Jesus into your wait, He anchors Himself as a strand that is constant throughout the entire braid. [9] He can't be removed. Now, you could try, but I think we all know what happens when we decide to cut our own hair. You might remember getting some practice when you were younger by testing your scissors out on your Barbie doll, sibling or pet. We all know how that turned out. It's a job best left to the professionals.

When you begin to braid your emotions, you now intertwine Jesus with each strand. Eventually you'll start to see how He brings in new strands of emotions you hadn't experienced during your season.

He starts intertwining your heartache with hope. And then you pick up more strands that now might consist of grief and glory. As you continue, He mixes your isolation with illumination. By the time you are done with your braid, all those thoughts and feelings are mixed in one beautiful story pulled together by Jesus. When you step back and look at what you just created, the picture looks different because of who you invited into it.

Throughout that process, He's working in and through you to make your wait valuable, transformational, and hopeful.

I had a choice that day I was picking up sticks in my yard. Up until that point, I had used those twigs as a way to protect myself from the true pain this season of waiting had brought into my life. As a way to avoid acceptance and to shield myself from the outcome I feared most, I buffered myself from the growing pains this experience could bring and safeguarded myself from truly having to sit and taste the sourness of what I was going through.

After building a barrier for two-and-a-half years, I was getting pretty good at it, if I do say so myself!

But that day my heart was finally open, and I invited Jesus into my wait. He revealed two options: I could continue constructing my walls, or I could use those sticks to create something beautiful.

I chose the latter and haven't looked back.

Stick by stick, Jesus helped me reconstruct what I had been hiding behind and started me on a new path that would lead to my biggest breakthrough, in more ways than one. The decision to build something beautiful continues more than four years later. Pause a second on that. You guys, what God started that day is still actively working all these years later. Praise God for his ability to move us in such a powerful and legacy-changing way!

FULLY LIVING

The story I was telling myself, the narrative I had on repeat for more than two-and-a-half years, revolved around one thing: becoming a mom.

Every waking thought, decision, schedule, and dream was centered around this. Consequently, every emotion was in limbo based upon what did or did not happen. It was the worst roller-coaster ride I'd ever been on and yet, I didn't know how to get off.

The idea of trying to rewrite what I was going through was never a thought in my mind. I was so focused on my outcome that nothing else mattered. I had blinders on and could only see life through the lens of getting my heart's desire.

My narrative changed the day I picked up those sticks in my yard. While my story still involved doing all I could to try and reach my desired outcome, it now also included, "How can I use my experience to help others and use my story to bring God glory?" My narrative was no longer only about me and what I wanted. It had expanded to include Jesus and help others.

Until Jesus helped me flip my coin, the only way my story would be complete and full, would be when my reality matched my expectation.

But Jesus says in John 10:10 – "I have come that they may have life and have it to the fullest."

When I first read this verse during our journey, I was a bit confused. My heart, feelings, and everything around me screamed my life is not full! How can it be when I have this gaping hole in my heart that I have no idea if or when it will be filled by what I'm praying, hoping, and believing in?

My expectation of a full life was dependent on the things I did or did not have. They became my standard of fullness. Do you have a similar expectation?

Hear me out. Our dreams and desires are healthy in and of themselves. The danger is when they become our only narrative and we try to go it alone without inviting Jesus in.

So often we tell ourselves, I can finally live when my desired outcome has arrived. This mindset often stops us from living where we currently are — with the mess and beauty right before us.

Yes, it's hard, and it's frustrating!

Yes, the heartache can be so intense some days it makes you catch your breath.

Yes, yes, and yes to all those thoughts and feelings you have or are experiencing with your current situation.

Thanks to Jesus, you're capable of having a full life while you wait. He wants you to know that you don't have to wait for your breakthrough to live life to the fullest. Notice I didn't say footloose and fancy free, or void of pain and suffering. When the feeling of a full life starts to change, it's an indicator of what we're relying on to create a full life. Earthly things will come and go, and while God wants us to make the most of our time here, those things ultimately aren't what give us a full life. The reason our lives are full is because of who's in it, Jesus.

There is no waiting for us to receive this full life. Jesus already gave it to us. It's instant, which is a relief for us who feel like the pause button has been pushed on our plans.

Jesus is saying you don't have to wait for your breakthrough to live life to the fullest.

"We can't change what we have experienced, but we can choose
how the experiences change us."

— *Lysa TerKeurst* —

— CHAPTER FIVE —

When the Outcome Doesn't Come

WHAT SHOULD'VE BEEN

The hardest part of any season of waiting is not having your longing fulfilled. It's easy to equate good when our prayer has finally been answered. But that's not something we're guaranteed.

We're all living in or will eventually face a situation in life that doesn't come to pass - being single, childless not by choice, or physical pain. It's a very true reality about life that has no words and makes my heart ache as I write this.

When we experience this loss, we're often left feeling:

- Abandoned
- Unworthy
- Forgotten
- Unwanted
- Lonely
- Unloved

As long as we live in the world, we'll experience suffering, sickness, heartache, loss, etc. This means bad things will happen to good people, and evil will continue to be a part of our lives. [10]

What is important for us to separate out is that bad things aren't from God, and He doesn't need them to create good in our lives. Remember, He's God and has the power to do anything. He created the Heavens and Earth, gave the blind sight, and raised people from the dead. Pure and simple, God is good.

Psalm 107:1 – Give thanks to the Lord, for he is good; his love endures forever.

James 1:17 – Every good and perfect gift is from above.

As painful as your current view might be, knowing this truth about God is powerful and brings back some control to your situation. Not your ability to guarantee your outcome but your ability to decide and choose how you're going to live in it.

I have no fancy or philosophical way to answer why some of us go through life with unmet desires. It's something I'll never understand. We can do all the right things and still not get what we want. We can and should take steps to give us the best chance of receiving these things, but ultimately, we aren't in control of the outcome.

And when that happens, we experience a loss.

It's an ache that never really goes away. It fades but will always be there. A big part of what you're experiencing is grief.

I used to think grief only happened when you lost someone. I now understand grief happens anytime you lose something — people, dreams, hopes, expectations, or plans you had for your life.

Living a life you never imagined is difficult. Your feelings are valid. They're yours and you have a right to them. I may not know your exact situation or the loss you are living in but know my heart aches for you.

I also want to share a truth about our outcomes that might sting a bit. You're welcome to absorb the sourness of it or spit it out. You choose.

Think of it this way. The world prioritizes outcome over process. Why? It's natural to prioritize the outcome because it feels better than focusing on the messy, painful process of life.

Often, we associate and tie our value, worth, and identity to an outcome. When it takes longer to achieve than we expect or it doesn't happen at all, we begin to doubt and second-guess ourselves. We get frustrated, and the waiting period is like adding fuel to the fire, making it worse.

But as I later learned, the things we experience in life, good or bad are just that, an experience. They're not where my identity comes from, God is.

What's important for us to separate out is that bad things aren't from God and He doesn't need them to create good in our lives.

Your outcome doesn't determine your identity.

I finally understood that life is more than just getting everything I want when I want it. My heart and relationship with Jesus are ultimately what He wants for my life, and these waits can be a catalyst for that change.

Our waits are called a season for a reason. Just like we have weather seasons that come and go throughout the year, our personal seasons will shift and eventually come to an end. The part we get hung up on, because we're human, is the length of them.

I live in South Dakota, and, trust me, I wish I could shorten our seemingly 9-month season of winter down to two. [11] But what gets me through our 30-below days is knowing that this weather will end and warmer days are ahead. That change might take much, much longer to arrive and look way different than I expected. Like when the weather man says we'll get a light dusting of snow, and I wake up to a foot of it! Regardless of the inaccurate forecast, I know a change is coming.

While we aren't entirely in control of our outcome, we can control how we choose to live our lives in the in-between. It may not look like anything we imagined, but this doesn't mean we need to lose all hope in life and Jesus. In fact, He's the only reason we can have it. You are more than just your outcome.

THE IMPORTANCE OF HOPE

Let's be real. When you feel stuck in a situation for any length of time, it can feel impossible to have hope. At times, it may even

Your outcome doesn't determine your identity.

feel childish to keep believing and trusting in something that you have no physical affirmation of happening.

You know the reason it can feel like that? Because our hope is in something that is ever-changing, it shifts like a leaf in the wind based upon whether our desired outcome is received. If our journey to our end result is changing and our hope is in that alone, it makes sense why our level of hope would change, too.

I think hope is often thought of as this lofty idea that seems to float above us, out of reach, yet constantly dipping in and out of our sightline. It can seem impossible to obtain or hold on to.

But hope is so much more than a feel-good aspiration. It's sustaining.

It's the very thing that keeps us going and gives us strength when we feel like our plans have been postponed.

Regardless of sight or affirmation, when we put hope in something that's constant, our hope can be stable, secure, and immovable.

Why is hope so important?

Without it, we lose our confidence in others, ourselves, and God.

Hope is the little engine that could, pushing us to confidently wait in expectation. It's the one thing that inspires us to keep going, despite our feelings or circumstances. Hope never changes. It sustains us and is not based on obtaining our outcome.

Hope is important to Jesus because it's who He is. He's the very definition of hope. Through Jesus' death and resurrection, He became the hope of salvation for all mankind. The whole world thought He was gone, but three days later, He rose from the dead. Because of that, we have hope.

I want you to have hope in your wait because for so long, I didn't.

I allowed my hopelessness to take control and take away so much of my life because I didn't have the outcome I wanted. I was staring so long at the one side of my coin, wishing and hoping for it to change instead of flipping it over and finding a whole new way of living. All because it wasn't what I had planned.

Hope is important to Jesus because it's who He is.

"It's imperative that our desire for God outweigh our desire for what He can give us. It's about who He is, not just what He can do."

— Caleb Stanley

I want more for you during your wait. And so does Jesus.

Jeremiah 29:11 - For I know the plans I have for you, declares the Lord, plans to prosper you and not to harm you, plans to give you hope and a future.

Romans 5:3-4 - Not only so, but we also glory in our sufferings, because we know that suffering produces perseverance; perseverance, character; and character, hope.

It's so easy to think we have no control over what we do during our wait, because we're only focused on doing what will get us what we want. But, it's not a one-way street. There are many things we can do that ultimately can deepen our relationship with God and bring us growth. This is exactly what He desires for us during our wait.

Remember this, Jesus wants something from us just as much as we want something from Him.

"Obedience is not measured by our ability to obey laws and principles; obedience is measured by our response to God's voice."

— *Bill Johnson* —

— CHAPTER SIX —

Are You Gonna Go My Way?

FAITHFUL OBEDIENCE

For much of my life, I've been a rule follower. I see rules as guardrails making the path of life much easier to follow, most of the time. Some of it has to do with the fact that rules typically have pre-determined outcomes.

I often viewed obedience as following the rules. Doing the right things according to the guidelines outlined by religion and government.

- Following The 10 Commandments
- Going to church every Sunday
- Praying before every meal
- Not running a red light
- Silencing your cell phone at the movie theatre
- Filing my taxes on time

Most of us are obedient to these rules because we know the consequences and are afraid of what would happen if we don't follow them. Most rules come with outcomes that are known.

But when life hits a season of waiting, that all goes out the window. There are no rules, and that's when being obedient takes a different turn. Being obedient to these concepts is a different story:

- Believing before seeing
- Living life as if you already have the very thing you're missing
- Believing in something despite no affirmation of it actually happening
- Changing directions because of God's nudging

All throughout Scripture, we see stories of people, just like you and me, acting in obedience.

When it didn't make sense.

When it seemed impossible.

When everything they saw or thought they knew told them otherwise.

I thought I was pretty good at this obedience thing until I realized, it's more than just the things I do or don't do. Obedience is also our willingness to surrender our plans and follow God's, despite being afraid, feeling inadequate, or not knowing how or why.

This type of obedience is harder to follow because there's more uncertainty associated with it. The outcomes are unknown. Ultimately, this type of obedience takes your relationship with God to a whole new level. Obedience at this level requires faith, taking risks, being uncomfortable, and stepping outside ourselves.

Obedience is also our willingness to surrender our plans and follow God's, despite being afraid, feeling inadequate, or not knowing how or why.

I truly believe our ability to live in the wait runs parallel with obedience. The reason why is because for us to find value and deem our waiting seasons as transformational, it requires us to agree to the very things God is asking us to do.

And many times, they look much different than what we think they should. If you're anything like me, the last thing I want to do when my life is feeling out of control and not going according to plan, is follow a direction that seems counterproductive to what I think.

While we had our whole life planned out – oh wait, that's just me – it doesn't allow or require us to be obedient because, in theory, we already are. It's just that we're being obedient to ourselves and our plans.

Being obedient to God during our wait requires a bit more from us, and that's where faith comes in. That's the only way it can work. We step out in faith to be obedient to the crazy, bold, big things God is asking us to do because of the confidence we have in Him, not ourselves.

What I've found with obedience is that it's a process. It takes a relationship to build it. For many of us, the idea of following or listening to someone we don't really know isn't something we prefer to do. Our preference is to obey those we know, respect, and love.

With that, it seems pretty logical that one way to aid this process is by deepening your relationship with God. Truly getting to know Him allows us to trust Him and what He says about us and our lives.

A tangible way to do this is to reflect on all the times God has been faithful in your life to build up your confidence. Grab a sheet of paper and title it, "God's Bank of Faithfulness." Make a deposit by listing all the ways He's been faithful in your life. In what ways has He provided for you? That provision could include everyday, seemingly minor, take-for-granted incidences. Or maybe it's mile marker moments when your long-awaited prayers were answered.

God's Bank is open and available 24/7. That means whenever you feel yourself doubting or questioning His ability to perform a miracle, go back to the bank. Take out this list and make a withdrawal by reflecting on all the ways He's provided for you in the past. Even the times it took longer than you wanted, looked different than you pictured, or was more painful than you preferred. Use this as a reminder of how God can provide for you, even in this situation you're facing that seems impossible.

And remember this, God's faithfulness isn't solely determined by getting the things we want in life.

I'm going to let you in on a little secret. Obedience is not easy, but speaking from experience, it is worth it. It can create an entirely new dependence on God that will deepen your trust in Him more than anything else you'll experience. The peace you have is based upon who He is, not on your outcome or assurance of it happening.

It's much, much easier to be obedient to things we can visibly see, understand, and to which we know the rules and outcomes. But when God asks us to be obedient to things we can't see or make sense of, we often pause and question why. We can't comprehend or even begin to imagine how or why God could use such a thing for good. How could He use this crazy step to bring us closer to our desired outcome, when in our humanness, it seems like it's the opposite direction.

If you've ever been in an airplane before, did you ever notice how sometimes your flight takes you thousands of miles in the opposite direction of your planned location? It may take longer than you want, and you'll probably experience some turbulence, but you'll eventually arrive at your destination.

DIVINE INTERRUPTIONS

Where I live, it seems we have five seasons to our yearly calendar — spring, summer, fall, winter, and road construction. You're almost always guaranteed to run into some sort of detour, regardless of the time of year. While you might understand these improvements will enhance your driving experience at a later date, at the moment when you have places to be, it's nothing but an interruption. An unnecessary delay that's messing with your plans and is seemingly a waste of time.

However, I challenge you to think of these times, when life doesn't go according to plan, as a divine interruption. An invitation where God is asking you to use your time differently.

A nudging to look at your situation, beliefs, and mindset another way. We might not see these encounters as "divine" at the time they happen. But throughout your wait, God will begin to reveal the puzzle pieces He's so intricately been putting together, and you'll begin to see the new picture He's creating.

These disruptions take us off autopilot so we can rewrite the narrative from what I want to do, experience or have, to what God is asking of me and my time.

They're a visual reminder that invites us to pause.

If you're looking for a sign, this is it! Think of it as an internal stoplight. When a divine interruption happens, the light has turned red, telling us to stop. This creates space for us to look at the delays in life and ask different questions.

- "What is God wanting me to evaluate or change?"
- "How is God asking me to spend my time right now?"
- "What is God nudging me to focus on instead?"
- "How is God wanting me to use this time differently?

While waiting for the light to turn green, you and God get to decide your next move:

- Keep going the pre-determined path you set out to take
- Make a right or left-hand turn, moving you in a new and different direction
- Pull a U-turn and try again
- Choose to stay at the stoplight

Either way, these divine interruptions are calling us to evaluate the plan we meticulously organized for our lives vs. the path Jesus is wanting us to take.

It might look like starting over.

It might not make sense to anyone, even you.

It might go against recommendations and logic.

It might not get you to your outcome.

But because your agenda has been flipped from yours to God's, you're more curious to discover what these roadblocks can bring to your life vs. what they take away.

A divine interruption is an invitation where God is asking you to use your time differently.

Section 3

GUIDANCE AND GROWTH

"If your answer to prayer is delayed, it is gaining interest. And when breakthrough comes, it will come with a greater power and glory than if it had been released at the moment you first prayed."

— *Bill and Beni Johnson* —

— CHAPTER SEVEN —

The Truth Tree

LIVING IN THE WAIT

It was here, in my yard, picking up countless sticks over two-and-half years into our journey, I heard it.

I heard my heart.

It was not a moment to be mistaken or tossed carelessly into the wind that was blowing around me. I knew what was going on the instant it happened.

I had heard my heart, and it was here that God answered my question.

He told me, "I want you to *live* in the wait."

———————————

What I've found and learned from many of you is that waiting feels so passive, leaving you wondering, what can I do during this time? If I'm being encouraged to make the most of these middle moments, what does it actually look like?

Knowing we feel so out of control during seasons of waiting, our first and natural response is to find whatever we can control. The seven truths from The Truth Tree are exactly that.

They're what you can do during your wait, rooted in principles to encourage, grow, and refine your heart. They'll deepen your relationship with God, loved ones, and most importantly with yourself.

And yes, some of them may eventually open doors that will bring you to what your heart desires and an end to your season of waiting. It's not guaranteed. Remember, that's a job reserved only for Jesus. And for some, it will illuminate and lead your heart to new ideas, desires, and outcomes you would've never been open to had you not traveled that road of waiting.

We get to choose how we use the in-between times of life, and it starts with Living in the Wait.

This mindset allows you to put The Truth Tree in motion. Living is a verb, which means that, to do it, there has to be some sort of action on your part. And I'm not talking about the check-off the list, run through the motions type.

It has to be intentional, heartfelt, and surrendered action.

Choosing to live in the wait is different from what we prefer to do during these delays.

He told me, "I want you to live in the wait."

Let's be real, walking through a season of waiting puts us in survival mode because we feel threatened. The burden of carrying this unmet desire often leaves us wanting to protect ourselves from the pain this loss is creating. We just want to curl up and play dead. Remember, waiting is a loss of control and typically seen as a waste of time, a passive place of nothingness, standing in the way of our final destination. It makes sense why taking an action counter-intuitive to the ideals of waiting aren't on our radar.

However, when we focus on Living in the Wait, it allows us to stay present.

To limit the rabbit holes we fall down where we think and fear the worst. This will happen. We're human, and I argue that letting ourselves spiral every now and then is healthy. It's our way of preparing and protecting ourselves. We're setting ourselves up for failure if we think this won't happen. We aren't trying to avoid, push down, or stuff away the thoughts and feelings we're experiencing, but rather accept where we are, own our story, and find the hope this new way of living brings.

The whole idea is to use this time differently. To use this space as an opportunity to be transformed by your wait.

These truths are what help you live in the wait and allow you to:

- Change the view of your situation from earthly to eternal
- Focus on who you're becoming in the process
- Reflect on what you're gaining
- Accept where you are, even if it's not where you want to be
- Surrender control over your outcome

Ultimately, the Truth Tree changes how you experience yourself, others, and God during your wait.

I've often wondered why it took Jesus two-and-a-half years to bring this message to my heart. It's not like He didn't have plenty of time to interject this idea into my life.

I now know.

It wasn't Him; it was me.

I wasn't ready.

This might be true for you, too, and that's ok. You can't force yourself to be ready to receive the message Jesus is preparing for you. What you can do is pray that He would soften your heart to be open to it.

I believe that if Jesus had presented this idea to me a year prior, even six months earlier, I would not have been open to receiving what He had to share. My heart would've been closed off to receiving the glorious, redeeming, and life-giving things God had in store for me. He would've been talking to me, and I would not have been listening. It would be like me trying to give you a compliment when we're in an argument. You're not going to

Ultimately, the Truth Tree changes how you experience yourself, others, and God during your wait.

be open to receiving kind words from me because we're mad at each other. Your heart isn't willing to hear what I have to say. It would literally go in one ear and out the other.

The same is true for God. He loves us enough that He'll respect where we currently are in our wait and lovingly take His time to give us the right message, the right word, when we're open and ready to receive it. He knows us that well. That, my friend, is the example of someone who truly loves, cares, and knows you.

Our hearts have to be open to let God take control and direct our steps to make sure whatever goal He has in mind is achieved during our seasons of waiting.

All I can say is that day in October, my heart was ready and willing, and that's all Jesus needs to plant a seed and direct us to be obedient to Him.

I remember a car ride during Christmas, a few short months after we learned we were expecting. Ry asked me if I had a deeper appreciation for this gift and if my parenting would change because of our journey. I quickly responded, yes. I told him, I couldn't go through such a difficult experience and not be changed.

These periods of pause have the ability to change our lives.

While we typically don't get to choose the theme of our wait, we do get to choose how we walk through it. Values, boundaries, and priorities may change, but the benefit of those adjustments can create a new legacy you never would've had, if it weren't for your season of waiting.

The wisdom you obtain when you're in the middle is filtered through your situation. This hard-earned insight can only be gained by living through it.

If you would've sought this same type of wisdom outside of your wait, it wouldn't have been the same or as life-changing. And I challenge none of us would be open to it. When life is running smoothly, we don't see a need to make adjustments, much less take the time to learn new things. Life is good, I don't need more wisdom.

But we stand to gain the most during seasons of waiting.

Why?

We're more vulnerable, resulting in open-hearts and a thirst-quenching need for help. These transitions times create a willingness to search for answers to solve our heartache.

I'm not sure what expectation or idea you had when you started reading this book, nor the exact season of waiting you're experiencing.

But I do know, Living in the Wait is not linear.

It's not void of negative emotions.

It's not about making lemonade out of lemons.

None of those are sustainable or real.

It's actually about taking those lemons and fully tasting them in all their sourness. Letting it fill every crevice of your body and only after we've truly sucked and tasted all the lemon has to offer, gently lay it back down and ask God,

"How can you use my story for your glory?"

What that looks like, none of us know, but as you put these strategies into practice, you may begin to see a pattern or feel a tug toward the very things your wait is preparing you for.

Maybe it's everything, exactly as you hoped for.

Maybe it's nothing you imagined and heartbreaking.

Maybe it's something even better, more beautiful and fulfilling than you could've ever dreamed.

Let's go back to The Truth Tree.

We stand to gain the most during seasons of waiting.

The Truth Tree

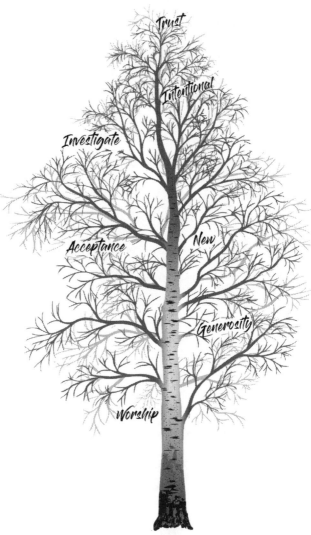

Trust

Intentional

Investigate

Acceptance

New

Generosity

Worship

"I am the vine, you are the branches."
John 15:5

"God works through you according to your level of faith.
Your praise and thankfulness are your level of faith: praise precedes
the victory."

— *Unknown* —

— CHAPTER EIGHT —

Worship

PRAISE PRECEDES THE VICTORY

Music has been a part of my life since I was little girl. I remember pushing the 8-track of "Rockin' Robin" by Bobby Day into my parent's 1976 Chevy Laguna. We'd blast Juice Newton and "Monster Mash" by Bobby "Boris" Pickett on their record-player and dance around the house. Mix in some Phil Collins, Amy Grant, and Garth Brooks and that describes the type of music I grew up with. Best part is that I now get to pass the gift of music to my daughter, who happens to also love Juice Newton.

That love for music became a lifeline for my faint heart during our wait. I needed it to help me express my thoughts and feelings when I didn't know how. They were my words when I had none. Music, the songs I listened to over and over, became my cry to Jesus. There's power in music. So powerful, it can bring healing.

"Music allows us to create an emotional narrative between the past and present when we struggle to articulate such a narrative in words. Its familiarity comforts us when the future seems unclear. It helps reconnect us to our identities and in so doing, helps bolster our resilience in the face of difficulty." [12].

I often thought worship, specifically through music, was something only reserved for when life was full of sunshine and rainbows. When I was in a place of being fulfilled with all my heart's desires. Makes sense, right?

It's easy to sing and dance when you're feeling happy-go-lucky. When you're distraught, broken-hearted, and your body is physically exhausted from the burden you've been carrying, not so much.

Come to find out, worship is simply one way of communicating with Jesus. It's praising who He is. The praise precedes the victory, and that's what worship helps facilitate.

I know from our earthly viewpoint this seems backward. How can I cry out in praise and thankfulness when I'm still waiting for the very thing I want to be thankful for in the first place? I get it. This thinking is what happens when we view our situation from the world's viewpoint. The Bible says, "My ways are higher than your ways." [13]. This line of thinking is so beyond our ability to comprehend, but that doesn't make it untrue.

I share this to give you permission to worship Jesus with every tear, pain, and loss you're experiencing. To not judge yourself or only reserve it for when you're feeling happy inside.

Sure, we can worship when we land the job, get married, have children, etc., but worship isn't only for when life is going according to plan.

After the season of waiting we experienced, I argue worship is even more important when we're faced with a roadblock.

Why?

Because every fiber in our being is telling us NOT to worship. Not to go to God. Not to cry out to Him. Not to be honest with Him. What we feel during our wait is the opposite of what we often think worship is, so we don't do it. And that can prohibit us from Living in the Wait.

For many, worship may look like reciting old hymnals, redundantly repeating phrases or words commanded by a pastor. If that was your experience, it makes sense why you aren't too jazzed about it. Or maybe you think it's hands raised, swaying, having a complete out-of-body experience. The pendulum of those experiences can swing pretty far.

But the most important question for you to answer is this, "What does worship look like for me?" How do I best like to communicate with Jesus?

Worship is intimate. It is about you and your relationship with God. It's a direct relation of what God means to you. It's an expression of your relationship with Him, so I get how it could feel a bit intimidating.

But know this, there is no wrong way to worship. Each of us has a unique relationship with Jesus because of who He made us to be, so it makes sense the way we worship and our comfort level with it, would also be different.

Push aside any judgment, or preconceived expectations of what you "should" or "shouldn't" do while you worship and explore it with your friend, Jesus.

"Acceptance doesn't mean resignation. It means understanding that something is what it is and there's got to be a way through."

— *Michael J. Fox* —

— CHAPTER NINE —

Acceptance

ACCEPTANCE OR RESISTANCE

I'll admit it. I tend to overcomplicate things... sometimes. Is it just me?

Honestly, it's a defense mechanism.

If I make or keep something complicated, it provides me an excuse to not have to work through it. To not have to do the hard work. To avoid the pain.

Yes, sometimes it seems easier to stay stuck than do the work to change or figure out a new or different way through it. It seems easier to stare at the one side of the coin.

Acceptance is one of those things. Because when you break it down, when we are in the wait, we are either living with acceptance or resistance. It's the awareness of what is vs. what we hoped for or expected.

When we are in the wait, we are either living with acceptance or resistance.

Think of it this way. Either you have your pants on, or you don't. Yes, you may have one pant leg on, but that doesn't mean you actually have your pants on. There is a difference. Often, I think we try hard to make something that it isn't because we desperately want it to be that way.

Looking back, I can clearly see I was living with resistance. I was focused on changing my reality instead of working through it. It wasn't until I picked up those sticks in my yard that I started living with acceptance.

When we're living with resistance, it ultimately steals the opportunity to live in the wait.

Living with acceptance brings a sense of contentment, peace, and readiness to move forward vs. wishing it never happened in the first place. It changes our perspective on the situation to be open to asking the question, "How can God use my story for His glory?"

A layman's terms way of thinking about it is adopting a growth mindset, which focuses on the growth that can be experienced rather than the struggle it's created.

It takes discipline to live with acceptance because you are making a conscious decision to know what you don't have control over. And despite not being okay with it, you believe you can move forward.

Hear this, acceptance does not mean you like, agree, or are okay with what you're going through. Instead, you're trying to find ways to live through it, instead of ignoring it.

Acceptance is trying to find ways to live through your reality, instead of ignoring it.

For me, that's the key to really understanding what it's like to live with acceptance. Because for so long, my feelings didn't match what I thought it should feel like to live that way.

And here's the thing with acceptance. When we invite God into the equation, He has a way of changing our ability to live through our reality.

For me, it happened when I finally realized I was more than my outcome. I wasn't okay or happy with my situation, but I no longer was trying to fight it, question it, ignore it, or wish it away.

Before we move on, it's important to note that this process of living with acceptance may continue to intertwine with conflicting emotions. Your frustration, disappointment, and anger will sit next to patience, purpose, and acceptance. And that's okay. It's a coexistence of trauma and a desire for healing.

Living with acceptance is difficult. Scratch that, seemingly impossible. It took me two-and-a-half years to get to that point. An even after that, it was a daily decision I had to make consciously, continually, and intentionally.

So, while the concept of living with acceptance vs. resistance may be simple, the act of living it out is anything but.

Here's one practical way to put this into practice: trade your negative beliefs with healing beliefs.

These are the thoughts and conversations we have with ourselves daily. Y'all know I'm not the only one who talks to myself, right?!

Focus on replacing the negative belief vs. criticizing yourself for having it in the first place. That's not productive, helpful, or showing compassion to yourself.

I challenge you to say and repeat these statements, even if you don't feel or fully believe them, yet.

NEGATIVE BELIEF	HEALING BELIEF
"I'm a failure."	"I'm doing the best I can."
"This is all my fault."	"I made the best decision I could with the information I had at the time."
"This is too much for me to handle."	"I'm capable but it's also ok to ask for help."
"I'm not worthy of receiving my heart's desires."	"I have value, I matter, no matter the outcome."
"I must've done something to deserve this."	"I don't like what I'm going through. I hate it, it's not okay, and I wish this wasn't happening, but I accept it as part of my story and I want to move forward."

"Be clever and curious just like a cat. Ask lots of
questions about this and that."

—*Sandra Magsamen*—

— CHAPTER TEN —

Investigate

INVESTIGATE = ADVOCATE

I grew up watching Inspector Gadget and Scooby Doo. In these shows, there's typically some sort of mystery to solve. The cast takes clues and asks countless questions to get to the bottom of what's really going on. By the time the show is over, they've discovered what was missing and solve the case.

If only we could close the case on our seasons of waiting in a matter of 30 to 60 minutes.

Nonetheless, there are parts that can be very similar.

When we're waiting for the desires of our heart, our lives can often feel like a mystery. We take clues from around us, past experiences, and God to crack the case on who, what, where, when, and why is causing us to stay stuck in this holding pattern.

In our need to control, we tend to overestimate our ability to find the missing clues. In fact, real life often has a much more complicated plot line than most mystery shows. But all hope is not lost as we do have control over our ability to investigate as much as we can about our situation and ourselves during the journey.

When you advocate for something, you are risking comfort for the chance at change.

Let's deploy our Go-Go Gadget Minds to dig into the third truth about Living in the Wait. (14)

When I think of the word investigate, the word advocate comes to mind. To me, they're one and the same. Investigating involves research and asking questions, which is exactly what advocacy entails.

A few synonyms for advocate are supporter, champion, and promoter. Be proactive. Educate yourself and be informed. Invest in your well-being and trust your gut. Speak up and ask questions.

While I understand there are many things in life we can't control, we do have the power to make choices and learn things to help us on this journey. Be your own advocate!

When you advocate for something, you are risking comfort for the chance at change.

This mindset applies to any area of your life. Think about it, who wouldn't want to be a supporter, champion, or promoter of their mind, body, time, relationships, and spirit?

The main reason it's so important to be your own advocate, is because truly, no one else will.

It's your health, your life, and you have ownership in it. You may not always be in control of the outcome, nor what chooses to come in or out of your life. But, it's up to us to be informed. Our body, mind, and spirit are our responsibility.

When it comes to your style of advocacy, be consistent with who you are, but know that to create change, it's probably going to be bit uncomfortable at first. This was definitely true for me, but as the months passed I began to realize I needed to be more proactive to be informed. My health, marriage, life, and future baby were the only reminders I needed to sacrifice my comfort and start advocating.

It may take time to learn and be comfortable advocating for yourself, and that's ok. Be persistent, and over time, it will get easier.

So, let's get tactical + practical about how to advocate in your own life.

KNOWLEDGE IS POWER
Do your research ahead of time. While it is important to be informed, be cautious about the information you are processing. Is it from trusted sources? Do you know others who have found similar information? What sites do people you trust recommend?

DON'T ASK, DON'T GET

Asking questions often leads to an epiphany or redirection. Do so boldly, confidently, and repeatedly. Do not be afraid to ask, and do not apologize. There's a lot at stake, so own the opportunity and be informed by asking questions. You don't know what you don't know, so ask and ask again. This includes asking yourself questions to dig deeper into how you're really feeling and holding up during this season. Investigate yourself as part of the growth process.

TALK TO OTHER PEOPLE

Sharing every detail isn't necessary but it can be so helpful to get pointers from others who have walked a similar path. Yours may not be the exact same, but you'll start to find similarities, which may be applicable to your situation and makes the experience less isolating. Talking to others can even accelerate the learning process saving you time, money and resources. Even if it's only one person, their very presence can give you the permission to exhale the stress of what you've been holding onto. Trust me when I say it's worth the risk of being vulnerable.

TRUST YOUR GUT

When something doesn't feel right or doesn't fall in line with your values, assess what's underneath that feeling. Pause to do a heart check to see how you're truly doing and feeling about the path you're on or the decision you're about to make. Your feelings connect you to a need. How's your body responding physically? Trust that gut feeling when it's time to get a second opinion, go a different direction, step out in faith, or stop.

You may not be able to explain it, but trust yourself to make the best decision knowing you're doing all you can to help your situation.

RISK BEING SHUSHED

There's a story in the Bible that addresses the very topic of advocacy. It's about a blind man found in Mark 10:46-52.

A blind man, Bartimaeus, was part of a large crowd. He began shouting when he heard Jesus was coming. Many in the crowd rebuked him, telling him to be quiet.

And yet, their disapproval made the blind man shout even louder. The crowd's reaction didn't cause him to stop. He knew in his heart what he needed to do. He knew he stood to lose the opportunity to gain his eyesight, if he decided to listen to the crowd and stop shouting for Jesus.

How often do we have an idea, situation, decision, or prayer that gets shushed by the crowd? That crowd could be friends, family, professionals, strangers, even ourselves. This creates a chain reaction of doubt in our hearts and, instead of trusting the spark we felt, we start telling ourselves things like:

- It's too big a prayer.
- This is impossible.
- I'm wasting God's time by asking for this.
- This will never work.
- Who do I think I am trying to do this?

Risk trying because you know what's at stake, and you know what you stand to gain.

You name it, I'm sure many of us have either thought it or said it. I can think of many times I've allowed the risk of ridicule, embarrassment, or looking small, stop me.

The biggest crowd I'm up against is me, myself, and I.

Maybe I'm the only one, but I have consistent negative beliefs constantly yelling at me. Sometimes it seems like I have to shout over them to send my prayer request to Jesus. Can anyone else relate to this?

I think the blind man's perspective is so important when we're waiting because that time in life is full of uncertainty and we're extremely vulnerable.

Many crowds will try to shush us about a decision we're making, a procedure we're doing, think we're overreacting, question the way we're handling situations, or judge our reaction to grief and loss. They might mean well, but ultimately, it creates doubt in our hearts, and we stop shouting our requests to God, believing in a miracle, and having hope.

Imagine instead what life would look like if you approached things the way the blind man did - if you didn't let the crowd mute your voice.

The blind man spoke up and received his sight. You guys, that's huge! He knew what was at stake if he decided to listen to the crowd instead of shouting for Jesus. He was willing to risk ridicule (maybe even worse) in hopes of being healed by Jesus. WOW.

Speaking up could be advocating for your health, job, or marriage. It could be taking the class, starting a business, switching treatments, or calling an estranged loved one to say I'm here. Maybe it's repeating the same prayer request for years on end, even if you don't see a change. For some, it may mean choosing your health and well-being over others.

Prior to my season of waiting, I wouldn't have had a need or desire to step out with this type of faith. I had no reason to take this sort of risk until I was forced to risk everything I had.

I urge you to be like the blind man. Take that risk, and speak up. There are going to be many people who try to shush us, most likely because it makes them uncomfortable. Risk trying because you know what's at stake, and you know what you stand to gain.

"For I am the Lord your God who takes hold of your right hand and says to you, Do not fear; I will help you."

— *Isaiah 41:13 NIV*—

— CHAPTER ELEVEN —

QUESTION MARK OR PERIOD

It's one thing to trust God when life is going according to plan, ahem, I mean my plan. It's a whole different thing to trust God when it's not.

The best explanation I've found addressing this comes from *Unscripted* by Ernie Johnson, Jr. There are two pivotal points he shares that radically changed the way I trust God. Specifically, a conversation Ernie had after he was diagnosed with cancer.

The first is a quote from Ernie's pastor, "You're asking the wrong question. It's not why this happened, but how God is going to use it for His glory." [15]

Big gulps.

Asking this question takes our wait from earthly to eternal.

What question have you been asking?

I ask to get you curious about how you've been living in your wait. Not to judge or condemn, but to love you. Because remember, I was asking that very question, "Why, God?" for two-and-a-half years. So, I'm right there with you.

I want to trust Him even if the plan I want does or doesn't happen.

I can see how changing that question flipped my perspective. It was no longer about me, but God.

Easier said than done, but I learned it's about Him working the impossible in my life, which ultimately, will work the impossible in someone else's life. It's about Him working through me to bring others to Christ. To spread the power of hope and encouragement to others to allow Him to work through them during their wait.

I think asking that question, "Why, God?" is easier and less risky than asking, "How, God?" You might laugh at that idea, but here's why.

Asking God to show us how He's going to use our situation for His glory requires us to be open to change. To look at things differently and above all, invite God into our wait and be willing to be a part of the solution instead of blaming Him for our situation.

The second point is another quote, again, from Ernie's pastor, "This whole thing is about this: trust. Is it going to be trust with a question mark? Is it going to be 'I'll trust God if (insert whatever thing you are going through) comes back the way you want it to'? Or is it going to be trust. Period." [15]

What I realized was that I trusted God, but honestly, it was only when life was going according to my plan. It was, "I'll trust God if I get what I want, when I want it." And this delay wasn't according to my plan. Hence, my trust in God was shaken. My foundation slowly started to crumble and everything I thought I knew about myself, God, life, and faith was very foggy.

This life I had envisioned, planned, and, more importantly, expected to happen, wasn't.

Now what? What was I supposed to do with a plan that:

A. I didn't want
B. I wasn't prepared to deal with
C. Made me uncomfortable and caused me to question everything I knew

I wrote a journal entry years prior about this exact thing. I was telling God that if I knew why or had some sort of time frame to know, yes, my breakthrough will happen, I would be able to better accept what I was going through. I said, I know it ultimately comes back to trusting you and what your word says.

This journey made me re-evaluate what it means to genuinely trust God.

I think part of me knew I could trust Him because the things I trusted Him with I either received or understood. It was easy to believe when I got what I wanted and things went according to my plan.

This time around, trust means something different. I want to trust Him even if the plan I want does or doesn't happen.

While He always has the "best" in mind for us, we can have a different interpretation of what that means. For me, best usually means positive or basically getting what I want, when I want it.

For God, best is whatever brings Him glory and deepens our relationship with Him.

IT STARTS WITH PRAYER

Knowing we should trust God and actually doing it are two different things.

One of the most accessible ways to get on the trust train is through prayer.

In its simplest form, prayer is talking to God. It's striking up a conversation with Him. While simple in nature, when we use prayer, we're calling on the most powerful form of change. AMEN for those in the wait!

Being in conversation with Him creates trust, and that trust allows you to communicate with Him openly and honestly. Just start, even if it's feels awkward, difficult, or silly. Your feelings will eventually catch up.

Prayer taught me how to live in the wait because it brought me peace, relief, and, most importantly, hope, knowing that God was in control. While yes, He had the power to take away my wait, more than that, He had the power to transform my life for good through an extremely difficult experience.

The reason prayer may seem so hard is because we tend to overcomplicate things. So let me break it down into three simple ways.

PRAY UNFILTERED

Tell God *exactly* how you're feeling. Yes, exactly how you're feeling. He can handle it, but most importantly, He wants you to come to Him with a willingness to be raw and vulnerable.

He wants to see you. ALL. OF. YOU.

Talk to Him like you would a friend, except He's the type of friend that won't argue, dismiss, or abandon you. [16] He won't judge or say I told you so.

Instead, He can validate your experience because, as the Bible tells us, He knows exactly what you're thinking and feeling because He knows firsthand how difficult waiting is.

PRAY CONTINUOUSLY

Opportunities to be in conversation with God happen all the time, every day. It's up to us to see and use them as way to spend time in prayer.

He's always ready and available. It's usually us who puts up barriers to His accessibility.

My favorite way to do this is using the "down" moments my day. Like standing in line, doing dishes, folding laundry, brushing my teeth, sitting at a red light, you get the idea.

Those tasks eventually prompt your brain and heart to start praying because it becomes an intentional act you associate with the task. This approach allows you to have continuous prayer time with God, which keeps you connected to Him, and builds trust.

These can be quick, short words, or phrases.

- I trust you.
- Thank you.
- Please show me.
- Help me understand.
- What now?

PRAY EXPECTANTLY

You've heard it before: "I'll believe it when I see it."

This worldly mindset prioritizes seeing before believing. This requires zero faith because what you now believe is something you've already seen.

Often, I felt I was minimizing my prayers to God because I, in my human capacity, felt like they were impossible requests. I felt silly asking God for them, especially when my current circumstances proved and looked otherwise.

This all changed thanks to a recommendation from a friend. I listened to a sermon from Rick Warren about breakthrough prayer. In it, he references Mark 11:24 – "Therefore I tell you, whatever you ask for in prayer, believe that you have received it, and it will be yours."

The believing happens before anything you want to receive materializes.

You must believe you have it before you get it. The believing happens before anything you want to receive materializes.

Before this, my prayers were begging God to give me what I wanted, and I wasn't consistent with my request. After hearing this sermon, every day, three times a day, I said this prayer, "Thank you Lord for getting us pregnant this year."

At first, it felt totally awkward. I felt really silly thanking God for something I hadn't received. I often chided myself because I felt like I was coming to God with too big and too impossible of a request. All of that was a lie the enemy was trying to tell me so I'd stop expectantly praying.

It was a battle within my heart and mind to keep going because logic continually reminded me, I didn't have that which I wanted and I had no idea if I ever would.

As the days turned into months, that feeling entirely went away and I became more confident in my request and believed He would provide. My voice became stronger as I prayed these words out loud every day, despite having no physical evidence or reassurance of my request.

I started praying expectantly in May.

We received the humbling news of our pregnancy in September of that same year.

Learning and applying this was a mic drop moment. It literally changed my life. You know how you see the before and after pictures from house renovations? Yup, I've got a before and after picture of my faith once I started praying expectantly.

Praying in expectation changed my understanding of how we can boldly come to the throne of God with our prayers. This type of praying ultimately transforms our relationship with Him because we're thanking Him in advance for answering our prayers, despite what we feel or see. That creates a whole new level of trust with Him.

One day you'll find you've crossed over from tentatively leaning into this prayer, to wholeheartedly, no holding back, believing you have received before it's placed in your life. When you get to that point, you'll know because there will be a shift in how you think and feel about your wait. You're trusting in the One who can provide, which means you can focus on living life to the fullest, regardless of what you're waiting for.

"Live less out of habit, and more out of intent."

— Unknown —

— CHAPTER TWELVE —

Intentional

READY, SET, ACTION

Ever since Ry and I started dating, we would create some sort of yearly list. For my 30th birthday, Ry created a 30 for 30 List based upon one of our favorite TV series on ESPN. This love of list-making helped us live in the wait because it set our sights on what we could do and how we could live.

Our list of intentions was based upon what we enjoy and who Jesus created us to be. The same is true for you.

This might seem like an easy step to skip, but without being intentional about Living in the Wait, it won't happen.

Why?

Because the weight of your wait will slowly pull you out to sea. The land of hope will slowly fade, and you'll be surrounded by the endless view of heartache and defeat.

We must be intentional with our time and how we spend it and the thoughts we allow to invade our head and heart. We can control those things, but we must be deliberate in how we do it.

Being intentional = deliberate discipline.

And, there has to be some sort of accountability. Mark your calendar, set a reminder, put a sticky note on your mirror, tell a friend. It's does require some planning and obedience, but your hard work will pay off. Being intentional looks different for each person based upon their hopes, dreams, and personality.

Remember this, being intentional isn't about adding another thing to your "to do" list or something you "have to do." It's about the growth, experience, memories, and fulfillment that comes from the life you're creating in the wait.

COVERED IN COMMUNITY

Our natural tendency is to turn inward when we're in a season of waiting. Guilt and shame often tag along and we start to blame ourselves for not being able to get what we want. Society says we should have certain things in our lives based upon a pre-determined schedule and when we don't, we're left feeling embarrassed and isolated, thinking we're the only ones going through this.

So, we build another wall with our sticks to protect ourselves from further judgment and comparison.

But many hands make light work, and the same is true when it comes to being covered in community during the delays in life.

Community is more than a number's game. It's about finding one person you can trust. Someone with whom you can be vulnerable and who truly cares about you.

I feel so fortunate to have had lots of support from the community around me. Family, friends and complete strangers rallied around Ry and me. They consistently cared for us and were willing to help carry the weight of our wait. Being vulnerable with this season of our life was an important step in welcoming community.

When your life plans come to a halt, it's time to reach out to your community. Only you know those people in your life that are on standby saying, "How can I help?"

It's an intentional act on our part to start the conversation. I'll be the first to admit, asking for help or sharing the deepest parts of me with others is terrifying. Cue the fear of judgment and comparison.

But I'll also be the first to tell you, that once I stepped out in faith, and chose to be vulnerable and honest with others, I was instantly greeted with love and support. I felt seen and heard with a sense of freedom because I was no longer lugging this secret around by myself.

Bottom line, connect with one person in your circle that you feel safe with to start the conversation about your season of waiting. Don't delay, do it today.

If you're searching for community, you've got one person waiting right here for you.

Community is more than a number's game. It's about finding one person you can trust.

"For I am about to do something new. See, I have already begun! Do you not see it? I will make a pathway through the wilderness. I will create rivers in the dry wasteland."

—Isaiah 43:19 NLT—

— CHAPTER THIRTEEN —

New

NEW BEGINNINGS

We have seven full-grown trees in our yard — a mish-mash of oak, silver maple, and pine. But you know what tree I was picking up sticks from that October day?

Our one and only birch.

And do you know what these trees symbolize?

Rebirth, new beginnings, and growth.

You guys!

Of all the trees in my yard that I could've been picking up sticks from, it was our birch tree! This is a detail only our loving God could've orchestrated. I'm overwhelmed by His attention to all aspects of our lives.

My stick moment birthed a new purpose and passion. From my loss, God brought new life. That day, He and I started the process of turning my heartache and disappointment into something beautiful. [17]

I felt Him nudging me to share our story to help others. But I told Him, if waiting is part of our story, I want to get the most out of.

I did not want to waste my wait.

I wanted to squeeze every lesson out of this experience because I didn't want to do it again. My heart had to be open to let God take control and direct my steps to make sure whatever goal He had in mind during my wait was achieved.

Thus was born (pun intended), Living in the Wait. An online resource to encourage and give hope to those in a season of waiting. While mine was infertility, I understood that waiting is something we all experience in life. And I needed to know, "How do I live in the wait?" Come to find out, many of you have been asking a similar question.

From the moment God planted the seed in me to share our story through the creation of Living in the Wait, I knew what I was about to embark on was bigger than myself. That this journey was about a responsibility to steward the story God had given me. To be a vessel for God to carry out His plans here on earth.

In a way that only God could orchestrate, He combined my passions in new and different ways that were fulfilling, life-giving, and Kingdom focused. While I was still believing for my outcome of becoming a mom, He started filling my life with a new joy that I would've never been open to experiencing, let alone thinking about, before inviting Him into my wait.

I've journaled since I was in middle school. Something about the ability to put my thoughts on paper was so freeing and necessary to remember all the details about my day. Side note, I still have all those worn diaries sitting on a book shelf. I must say, it's rather fun to flip through them, reflecting on how life actually unfolded vs. the game of M.A.S.H. I played over and over. [18] Blogging brought back that same sense of healing journaling provided for me when I was younger. Sharing online gave me an outlet to have heart-level conversations on a larger scale to benefit others and connect with others wondering the same things.

My love for meeting new people is a ten on the Richter Scale. [19] With my website, I was connecting and meeting people from all over the world. I was invited into a very personal part of my readers' stories, and I continue to be humbled by this.

What I love most about events is the process of taking an idea and creating and coordinating steps to making it happen and seeing it all come together. Seeing things go from idea to action energizes me. The strategy and organization required to write, create, and schedule posts checked every one of those boxes. All this to say, God used me and the unique skills and abilities He created me with in a way that was so life-giving and something I would've never sought out on my own.

I'm a pretty conversational, play-it-safe kind of gal. But this experience wrecked me in the best way possible, opening a new door of possibilities that only God in all His goodness, faithfulness, and love could create.

What I found is that being open to something new during this time comes down to purpose and passion. The best explanation I've heard is:

- Purpose is about others
- Passion is about you

Connecting with your purpose and passion is asking, "How can this situation, this time in life be used to help others? The world? Me?"

Uncover the new purposes that are forming from your frustrations. What ideas, desires or unfulfilled needs are coming to the surface because of your wait? Think of it, many of the products and services we use today were formed from a frustration inventors and entrepreneurs turned into purpose.

Our bodies are designed to send us signals about how we are feeling and does so every day. If you are hungry, your stomach growls. If you are thirsty, your throat feels dry. Our body does the same thing when it comes to meeting our higher-level needs. There is a physiological response when we're working within a purpose or passion. We receive cues, signals from our sympathetic and parasympathetic systems. Those signals can come in the form of a dull urging, increased heart rate, or uptick in energy.

What that looks like can vary in size. Living with purpose and passion could be as simple as sending a text, making a phone call, mentoring others, or sharing encouraging posts on social media. It could be as big as building a ministry, creating a movement, or writing a book.

Your detoured life is a testimony that can show the way for others when they need to see perseverance, faith, and hope.

God brought my purpose to light when He nudged me to start Living in the Wait. He guided me to take my frustrations and use them to encourage others waiting for a breakthrough.

Trust me when I say my five-year plan did not include starting a business, connecting with people from all over the world, and writing a book. The only reason I'm talking to you today is because God took a hold of my heart, and I was obedient to His direction.

Living in the Wait with purpose and passion shifts your focus from what you're experiencing to how your season can be used differently. Your journey, your process of discovering this will bring new life, new motives, and new dreams that only God could weave together.

Your detoured life is a testimony that can show the way for others when they need to see what perseverance, faith, and hope look like.

"A generous person will prosper; whoever refreshes
others will be refreshed."

— *Proverbs 11:25 NIV*—

— CHAPTER FOURTEEN —

Generosity

GIVING = GAINING

At the heart of generosity is giving. Giving is generosity in action. To be generous with what we have, we have to give it away.

We often hear of being generous with our time, talents, and treasures, but what about the other resources we have? We all have different ways of being generous based upon the gifts God has given us.

- **Words:** The tongue has the power of life or death. [20] Generously share words of encouragement.

- **Grace:** Extend grace to someone, even if they don't deserve it. This is exactly what God did and continues to do for us.

- **Story:** Sharing your story could lead others to Christ or provide hope and encouragement for someone who really needs it.

- **Hope:** When we are full of hope, we only have one option... share with others! [21]

- **Prayer:** This includes your friends, enemies, and the person working at your favorite restaurant.

Giving is generosity in action.

Did you know one synonym for giving is open-handed? I like visuals and that right there is very powerful imagery.

When we are open-handed, we are better equipped to give to others, but it also sets ourselves up to receive. The opposite is true, too. When our hands are closed, it is more difficult to give to others, and also to receive. Here's where we dig deeper. This visual of open vs. closed represents more than just your hands. It also applies to your heart.

I know, your logical side might be thinking, if you give something away you have less.

Giving is about gaining, not losing.

The intent is not to give expecting something in exchange, but just know your generosity will not return void.

So much good can come from giving. Lives are forever changed when we show people we care, when we take the time to listen, and pray for them. That not only has a positive impact on them, but on you, too. And guess what? They in turn will spread that to someone else, and this beautiful giving train keeps chugging along.

One act of giving can change so many lives. That's why it's so important to give.

While giving might be the last thing on your mind while waiting, I encourage you try it. Shifting your focus away from your situation and toward others is powerful and has the ability to change your perspective.

I'd be remiss if I didn't share the discernment needed to give, but not at the expense of depleting ourselves. Giving is ultimately an expression of our love and relationship with God. We give because we want to express our love for God, not to drain ourselves.

Lastly, but most importantly, giving all started with Jesus and the life-changing gift given to us all when He died on the cross. He opened his hands to give His life so we could be saved. That is the ultimate act of giving.

GENEROSITY = ENCOURAGEMENT

I'm a major fan of encouragement. That's why I created E+DAY, a day set aside on the 14th of each month focused on spreading encouragement to others. [22].

I've been on the receiving and giving end of encouragement many times and can attest to its power. It can transform someone's day or even their life.

By definition, encouragement is the action of giving someone support, confidence, or hope.

You might be asking, "How can I focus my energy on encouraging others when I'm the one needing the encouragement? I'm the one who's entire life has been turned upside down."

I hear you. Stick with me.

The byproduct of encouraging others is that it encourages you. Which means, you have the power to start the cycle of encouragement.

Encouraging others breaks up the continuous thoughts of hopelessness and overwhelm you may be feeling day-to-day about your wait. It gets you outside your situation and flips the coin.

The whole emotional tone of a tough situation can be transformed through encouragement – the giving and receiving of it. Encouragement can provide strength to look ahead, which is exactly what those in the wait want.

Here are a few ways to put this into practice. Start small and see how you feel. Notice how your mindset changes as you find ways to encourage others.

- Once a month, share encouragement with someone you know or even strangers.
- Leave a note of encouragement on the packing slip sheet that goes inside your return packages.
- When depositing a check, leave a note of encouragement in the deposit envelope.
- While on the phone with customer service, ask them if there is anything they're in need of prayer for.
- Write a few words of inspiration on the receipt of your restaurant bill.
- Leave a sticky note on the mirror at a hotel room, locker room, etc.
- When returning a library book, include a small notecard with a hopeful message.

Giving is about gaining, not losing.

Conclusion

When our daughter started walking around the age of one, we'd take her outside to wander and explore. I noticed a trend in some of her favorite activities as she stumbled around our yard. Sure, she'd find some rocks, leaves, and a random bug, but you know what she loved picking up the most?

Sticks.

Here, before my very eyes, was the one thing I so desperately had longed for. She was now picking up the same kind of sticks I had stacked up, years earlier. And instead of throwing them in a pile, building a wall to protect herself, she was sharing them, and they were bringing her joy.

And now, they had brought something beautiful to me, too.

We saved one of the very first sticks she picked up and have it on display. At the time, it was just a souvenir, a gift she gave to my husband, but I can see now that God was nudging her to share that stick to serve as a reminder.

A reminder of what He can do during our seasons of waiting.

What brings me hope about these seasons now is that because of Christ, I have the confidence to live through them.

I now know where and whom to go to when I'm in the middle.

I have peace knowing I can grow during difficult times because of who God is and His power to bring any sort of good from it.

That hallway is going to lead me to a new story I could've never imagined. It's going to take me places I would've never gone had my wait not brought me there.

These times are meant to refine and transform us to be more like Christ so our story can be used as a testimony to guide and help others. [23]

I know how to use the delays in life differently.

God brought things full circle for me when I realized the redemptive magnitude of my season of waiting.

Picking up sticks that day in October will forever be an unforgettable mile marker on the timeline of my life. It changed my course: as a woman, wife, mom, and Christian. While I'm not sure I will ever say, "Thank you God for infertility," I can thank Him for the illuminating work He did through one of the most heartbreaking seasons of my life.

Little did I know, Jesus' nudging that day would put me on a path that brought about divine interruptions, a breakthrough in my prayer life, and a more fruitful life than I could've ever planned, scheduled or prepared for.

The way I was living my life prior to our season of waiting didn't leave much space for God to be a part of it.

Let's be real, it didn't leave room for Him period.

Having everything planned out in our lives doesn't allow Him in. For Him to do HIS work, HIS plan, and HIS will.

But when we focus on Living in the Wait, it makes room for God to come in and adjust our plans, in ways that are higher than ours and more than we could imagine.

The same is true for you.

The God who helped me live in the wait is the same God waiting and wanting to bring something into your life that will add a deeper layer to your character.

We all have desires that are unmet. Places we feel God has not listened, answered, or given us what we want. But I want you to remember this, He's always there, right beside you in the middle of it all. He's ready and waiting to plant a seed so your roots can grow deep in Him allowing you to bear fruit and experience great growth.

This time is such a delicate transition going from our deepest heartache into a new unknown. So sensitive that it needs to be respected.

I give you permission to remove any guilt, shame, judgment or pressure you feel to take what you read in this book and force yourself to apply it to your life when you're not ready. Go ahead and let that all go. I know and trust that God, who loves you so much, will remind you of the words you read here. When the time is right, He'll open your heart to receive what He has to share with you.

As we say goodbye, my prayer is that you fully know your season of waiting, despite its pain and heartbreak, is an open invitation from God to use the delays in life differently.

That the truths shared help you live in the wait and give you some direction as you navigate the middle.

God is always orchestrating, moving, and shifting things to bring new beginnings that were grown through this chapter in your life.

Not because God caused it, but because of how God worked through it.

Waiting is difficult, there's no way around that. But when we look to Jesus to find the value in our wait, He softens our hearts so our wait is no longer about us, but about Him and His glory.

Waiting is difficult, there's no way around that. But when we look to Jesus to find the value in our wait, He softens our hearts so our wait is no longer about us, but about Him and His glory.

Thank You

It's hard to find the words to express the gratitude I have for everyone who brought this book to life.

To you, the reader, I'm beyond grateful and humbled that you would take the time to read anything I write. I pray the words on these pages guide you to the One who put them there in the first place, Jesus.

To Throne Publishing and AAP members, I needed a process and a community to turn this idea into action, and you did that for me. This is a win for all of us with dreams of doing big things that seem impossible or crazy.

To everyone who edited, proofed and reviewed each page, your eyes and attention to detail are such a gift.

To those on The Wait List, thank you for trusting me to share your wait with the world. Know this, your desires matter. While it might not make sense right now, Jesus is with you, always.

To Val, you diligently and patiently helped bring the concept of Living in the Wait to life with your talented design skills. We wouldn't be here today without the visual foundation you created.

To all my friends and family, who reached out, checked-in, and shared their own personal stories of waiting, your words and presence were a light when the days felt dark. Your vulnerability showed me what bravery truly looks like.

To everyone who prayed for Ry and me, you brought us hope and healing and continually reminded us about the power of prayer and importance of covering oneself in community.

To the Living in the Wait community, thank you for believing in me and this message. For trusting me to share hope and encouragement during your seasons of waiting. I appreciate each and every one of you.

To Mom, my editor, encourager, and friend. I appreciate you more than I can say. You've been there for it all, ready with a listening ear, an encouraging word, and prayer. I'm so grateful I get to call you Mom.

To Dad, your random check-ins and hugs mean the world to me. While your words may be short and sweet, I know your big heart has been cheering and supporting me the entire time.

To Ry, thank you for saying yes to me each and every day. For trusting me to follow this dream, knowing its purpose and reach is bigger than us. I just love you.

To Crosbee, I thank God every day that I get the opportunity to be your mom. I'm so proud of you, and I'm eternally grateful I get a front row seat to your life.

To anyone I might've inadvertently missed, please know the impact you've shared isn't forgotten and I appreciate you.

To Jesus, I'm continually in awe of all you've done during one of my most difficult seasons. I've experienced growth I never knew possible and witnessed the depth of your love and grace like never before. Thank you for not giving up on me and for taking my right hand to help me, all day, every day.

Notes

1. I can't encourage you enough to read John 15:1-8. This verse has so much symbolism and straight up wisdom when we're in the wait.

2. The Israelites wandered in the desert for 40 years awaiting The Promised Land. Sounds like a pretty similar story many of us can relate to, minus all the sand. See https://www.christianity.com/wiki/bible/what-can-we-learn-from-the-israelites-wandering-the-desert-for-40-years.html

3. The Wait List is a compilation of requests from people like you and me, all sharing a common thread of you guessed it, waiting. No one wants to be on The Wait List, but I pray you find encouragement and see all the miraculous ways God works through you during that time.

4. Ephesians 3:20 NLT - Now all glory to God, who is able, through his mighty power at work within us, to accomplish infinitely more than we might ask or think.

5. Psalm 37:23 NLT – The LORD directs the steps of the godly. He delights in every detail of their lives.

6. Galatians 6:9 NIV - Let us not become weary in doing good, for at the proper time we will reap a harvest if we do not give up.

7. Interested in starting a relationship with Jesus? Start here: https://hutchcraft.com/following-jesus

8. In my younger years I signed up to be a hair model. One year, the stylists made a mistake and my hair turned

bright orange (think of the fruit) instead of a soft maroon/amber color. It took two rounds of dying my hair black by my aunt to get it back on track.

9. Ecclesiastes 4:12 NIV - Though one may be overpowered, two can defend themselves. A cord of three strands is not quickly broken.

10. One of my all-time favorite books addressing this is The Shack by William Paul Young.

11. Fact, we've had a blizzard on my birthday, April 14, the past few years. Don't let the frigid temps deter you from visiting. I'll have a hat, gloves, scarf and hot chocolate waiting for you.

12. See https://theconversation.com/music-helps-us-remember-who-we-are-and-how-we-belong-during-difficult-and-traumatic-times-136324#:~:text=Music%20helps%20to%20reconnect%20us,in%20the%20face%20of%20difficulty.

13. Isaiah 55:8-9 NIV - "For my thoughts are not your thoughts, neither are your ways my ways," declares the Lord. "As the heavens are higher than the earth, so are my ways higher than your ways and my thoughts than your thoughts."

14. One of Inspector Gadget's signature lines is, "Go, Go Gadget!", followed by the tool he wants to deploy to help solve the case. Watch an episode!

15. *Unscripted: The Unpredictable Moments That Make Life Extraordinary* by Ernie Johnson, Jr. is a must-read.

16. One of the best books I've read about praying is *Talking with God* by Adam Weber.

17. Isaiah 61:3 NIV - and provide for those who grieve in Zion— to bestow on them a crown of beauty instead of ashes, the oil of joy instead of mourning, and a garment of praise instead of a spirit of despair.

18. One of my favorite games growing up was M.A.S.H. I'd have page after page of playing this game, all designed to predict what your future life would look like. Hint, none of what it predicted came true! See https://mashplus.com/how-to-play-mash/

19. One of my strengths, based on the CliftonStrengths is Woo. This is an assessment tool that explains the ways you most naturally think, feel and behave. See https://www.gallup.com/cliftonstrengths/en/253676/how-cliftonstrengths-works.aspx

20. Proverbs 18:21 NIV - The tongue has the power of life and death, and those who love it will eat its fruit.

21. Romans 15:13 NIV - May the God of hope fill you with all joy and peace as you trust in him, so that you may overflow with hope by the power of the Holy Spirit.

22. E+DAY stands for Encouragement Day; I picked the 14th of every month because that's the date of my birthday!

23. 2 Corinthians 1:4 NIV - Who comforts us in all our troubles, so that we can comfort those in any trouble with the comfort we ourselves receive from God.

About Melissa

MELISSA VANDE KIEFT is the founder of Living in the Wait, an online resource created to guide those who find themselves in a period of uncertainty, wondering when their wait will end. Her writing encourages us to be brave to discover the details God is orchestrating and designing through every life experience.

She's known for her big heart and is a huge fan of encouragement, meeting new people, heart-level conversations, and thank-you notes. In her spare time, you'll find her tinkering with her smoker, Oz, exploring the great outdoors, or watching college sports with her guy, Ry, and daughter, Crosbee, the coolest person she knows.

An author, speaker, and all-around organizer, Melissa has almost fifteen years of event planning experience and enjoys all things related to logistics and details.

Find Melissa at www.livinginthewait.com and @livinginthewait or reach out to melissa@livinginthewait.com.

Dig Deeper

Dig deeper by downloading your Living in the Wait Guidebook.

www.livinginthewait.com/guidebook